Conversation Starters

for

Alice Hoffman's

The Marriage of Opposites

By dailyBooks

  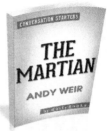

Tips for Using dailyBooks Conversation Starters:

EVERY GOOD BOOK CONTAINS A WORLD FAR DEEPER THAN the surface of its pages. The characters and their world come alive through the words on the pages, yet the characters and its world still live on. Questions herein are designed to bring us beneath the surface of the page and invite us into the world that lives on. These questions can be used to:

- Foster a deeper understanding of the book
- Promote an atmosphere of discussion for groups
- Assist in the study of the book, either individually or corporately
- Explore unseen realms of the book as never seen before

About Us:

THROUGH YEARS OF EXPERIENCE AND FIELD EXPERTISE, from newspaper featured book clubs to local library chapters, *dailyBooks* can bring your book discussion to life. Host your book party as we discuss some of today's most widely read books.

Table of Contents

Introducing *The Marriage of Opposites*

RACHEL POMIÉ WAS A REBELLIOUS CHILD, A DAUGHTER OF Jews who had fled from persecution until they found peace and prosperity on St. Thomas Island in the Caribbean under Danish rule. Her father started a business, exporting rum, sugar, and molasses, made from sugarcane, which was found in abundance on the island. Her mother was a member of the dreaded Blessings and Peace and Loving Deeds, an organization of women who did good deeds in the community but who were also responsible for making sure that the Jews on the island were kept under strict control.

Growing up, Rachel did not get along with her mother, who was controlling and believed in an inferior place for women. She did not encourage Rachel to look higher than what the restricted Jewish society allowed, an attitude that Rachel herself would later apply in her dealings with her own son, Camille Pissarro. She was best friends with Jestine, a West Indian girl, and daughter of the maid, whom she later discovered was her half-sister, since her father had had an affair with the maid. At the same time, desperate for a son, her mother adopted a child born out of wedlock, Aaron.

Rachel was married off in a marriage of convenience to Isaac Petit, a man thirty years her senior, in a bid to save the faltering business. She took to his children and treated them as her own. When Petit passed away, his family sent a representative to look after the business matters. Frederic came to St. Thomas, fell in love with Rachel, and they got married in spite of all the opposition. Since their union was believed to be incestuous, the Jewish community began to ostracize them.

During this time, Jestine fell in love with Aaron and had a daughter by him. Aaron was sent away to Paris when this came to light. He returned with a rich wife in tow. Unable to have children, the two stole Jestine's daughter and took her away to Paris.

Camille Pissarro grew up as a rebel, more interested in his painting than his schoolwork. He was sent abroad to France by his parents in a bid to make him stop painting and take more interest in an education. It did not work, and Camille began to study painting in Paris. When he returns, Rachel and Frederic want him to join the family business, but Camille is not interested. He went away to work on his paintings further in Venezuela, only returning when both his older brothers had passed away. In the end, Rachel decides to stop fighting Camille's profession and moves to Paris with him and Jestine, who wanted to be closer to her daughter.

In Paris, Camille falls in love with Julie Vellay, his mother's maid. This led to another major disagreement between mother and son. Frederic and Rachel never accepted this marriage, though Rachel got to know and love her grandchildren. It was in Paris that Frederic passed away, leaving Rachel alone. Jestine and Rachel were then together again like they had been as little girls.

Introducing the Author

ALICE HOFFMAN IS AN AMERICAN AUTHOR WHOSE BODY of work is versatile and encompasses a large number of themes. She has written books for adults, young adults, and children. Known for her dream-like and exotic settings, some of Hoffman's most recurring themes are love and loss, women's struggles and triumphs, historical fiction, and exploration of the Jewish life in history. She claims to be influenced by fairy tales and incorporates some of those elements into her work. She is also a screenwriter of some renown works and wrote the original screenplay of *Independence Day* (1983).

Born in New York City in 1952, Hoffman completed her schooling on Long Island and then went on to college at Adelphi and completed her BA. After this, she went to Stanford University and enrolled in the Creative Writing Center, from where she received her MA in creative writing. It was during her stint at Stanford that she wrote her first short story, "At the Drive-In," which was published in the literary magazine, *Fiction*. This was the first spark that led to her career as a writer and she began writing her first work,

Property Of, at the behest of Ted Solotaroff, the editor of *Fiction*. She later went to work at Doubleday, which published a couple of her books.

Hoffman's books have been translated into many languages, and some of her books have been made into movies, including the successful film *Practical Magic*. She has been feted by renowned publications such as *New York Times*, *People Magazine* and more.

On the personal front, Hoffman has suffered from breast cancer and was treated at Mount Auburn Hospital in Cambridge. She later helped establish the Hoffman Breast Center. She currently lives in Boston and is working on her latest novel.

Discussion Questions

. . . .

question 1

When she was a child, Rachel did not like her mother because she thought her too tough and heartless, trying to stifle her dreams. Why do you think Rachel herself began to behave in much the same way with her son, Camille? How and why do you think women in patriarchal cultures develop control issues?

. . . .

question 2

The author admits that most of the plots in the book are an invention. Which parts do you think are based on reality and which are an invention, and why?

question 3

The author claims time and again that Rachel lost her livelihood because women could not run a business or own property because of the laws that made life difficult for women. What do you think the author was trying to convey here? What were these obstacles against Rachel and/or her mother inheriting property? How could Madame Halevy be wealthy if this was the case?

· ·

question 4

The turtles that came to the shore and the story of the turtle woman are repeated a few times in the book. What do you think is the significance of this story?

· ·

. . . .

question 5

There are a number of superstitions that have been passed off as real in the book, especially about ghosts. Examples that stand out are the three crows when Frederic is about to die, and Rachel appeasing Isaac Petit's first wife and claiming she made things easier. Why do you think the author chose to base her narrative on superstitions rather than facts?

. . . .

. . . .

question 6

Camille, who had never been anywhere else, longed to escape the island while his father was happy to remain on the island even though he was raised in Europe and had traveled. Why do you think this was so?

. . . .

question 7

Rachel was fascinated by the folk tales of the island and wrote them down in her notebook. Which one of these tales did you like the most, and why?

. . . .

question 8

The Jewish women's association, Blessings and Peace and Loving Deeds,
kept a hawk eye on those who made a misstep, even if it was none of their
business. They justified it as "staying together because of persecution." Do
you think such control over personal matters by a religious/social
organization is justified? Discuss.

. . . .

. . . .

question 9

Rachel claims at the end that the rift with her son was because she loved him too much and that it was her own mother's revenge for Rachel that gave her grief. Do you think it was love or merely very bad parenting? Why would you want to change and control a child you claim to love like Rachel tried to do with Camille?

. . . .

. . . .

question 10

Both Jestine and Rachel blamed the "witch from Paris" for the abduction of Lyddie, Jestine's daughter; but they say nothing about Aaron himself, who did the actual dirty deed by paying men to tie up the mother and kidnap the daughter. Do you think this is because of internalized misogyny or because Aaron was Lyddie's father? Discuss.

. . . .

question 11

Though the Danish government had outlawed slavery, slaves were still found
on the island. Contrast the life and fate of slaves to those of the "free"
women. What similarities can you find in the way their lives were controlled
by others?

. . . .

. . . .

question 12

Camille had the bad luck to have two of the most unsupportive parents when
it came to his talent. Do you think he might have been closer to his family if
they had accepted him as he was? Do you think the two sides could have
worked out a compromise if his parents had not been so controlling and
stubborn? Discuss.

. . . .

. . . .

question 13

Camille's expenses were paid for by his parents, who finally realized he was not going to join the business while he painted. How can we ensure that talented people get the opportunity to follow their dreams without having to worry about their next meal? Do you think we should give people this opportunity? Why or why not?

. . . .

question 14

Madame Halevy was Rachel's mother's friend. She was also one of the women who made sure that no one stepped out of line in the Jewish community. She lived by the archaic discriminatory and controlling rules even when it was inconvenient to her. This was the reason she disliked Rachel, whom she thought of as a rebel. If this was so, why do you think she befriended Camille, who was not just a rebel but also an atheist?

question 15

A number of Jewish and European men had affairs with the Caribbean women and had illegitimate children with them. However, they did not marry these women and in some cases, did not bother to provide for them. Does this show "love" towards these women who were forced to live the lives of servants? Do you think Rachel's father really loved Adelle? Did Aaron really love Jestine? Discuss.

. . . .

question 16

New York Times reviewer, Hillary Kelly, claims that the alteration of Rachel into a bitter and angry mother is bizarre and wholly unbelievable. Do you agree with this? How do you think the story should have gone once Camille came into the picture?

. . . .

. . . .

question 17

Amanda Craig in her *Independent* review says that American authors excel at depicting marriage while the British are better at romance and children's books. Do you agree? Can you give an example of an excellent book on marriage written by a British author? Can you give an example of an excellent romance and children's book written by an American author?

. . . .

. . . .

question 18

The review in *NPR* by Jean Zimmerman claims that of all the colors
mentioned in the novel (and there are a fair few), haint blue is the most
important. Do you agree? Why or why not? How would you use haint blue in
your home?

. . . .

. . . .

question 19

In her review, Sandra McElwaine of *The Washington Times* claims that while the author portrays a veritable wonderland in the novel, the narrative tends to get overwhelmed by her lavish prose. Which parts of the story do you think could have been explained better in the place of excessive description and symbolism?

. . . .

. . . .

question 20

Reviewer Rebecca Steinitz of *The Boston Globe* calls the depiction of the four black women in the book (Jestine, Adelle, Lydia, and Rosalie) tired stereotypes of black women who cook delicious meals, sew beautiful dresses, and surround the white woman (Rachel) with love and support. But they do not stand up for their rights and the rights of others the way white women do. Do you agree with this statement? How would you have liked to see the Caribbean women depicted in the context of this novel?

. . . .

  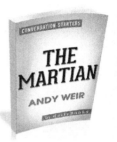

. . . .

question 21

The review by Martha Sheridan in *The Dallas Morning News* claims that Hoffman's work is a work of art because the purpose of art is to convey the truth of a thing, not to be the truth itself. Do you agree? Do you consider this book a work of art? Why or why not?

. . . .

. . . .

question 22

Kirkus Reviews claims that it is a pleasure to read this book because of the characters who are "willing to do anything for love." Do you agree? Why or why not? If you liked the book, what attracted you the most? If you disliked the book, what did you dislike the most?

. . . .

. . . .

question 23

Evie Saphire-Bernstein of the *Jewish Book Council* says that Hoffman's message is that the people and ghosts we are running from are who we eventually become. Do you agree? Why or why not? What other messages can you glean from this novel?

. . . .

. . . .

question 24

In *The Washington Post*, reviewer Wendy Smith claims that the final
revelation provides a bravura climactic twist. Which revelation do you think
Smith is referring to? Why do you think it would irritate readers?

. . . .

question 25

The Jewish Chronicle featured a review by Jennifer Lipman in which Lipman claimed that the lovers are more soap-opera protagonists than Romeo and Juliet, and the author's attempt to draw a connection between Pissarro's childhood and his future as a radical artist feels forced. Do you agree with this statement? What do you think the reviewer meant by "soap-opera protagonists?"

. . . .

question 26

Hoffman wrote adult novels for more than 20 years before she began to write for children. Why do you think it took her so long to start exploring fresh ground? Is writing for children more difficult than writing for adults, according to you? Why or why not?

. . . .

question 27

Hoffman's books are all rich in magic, folklore, and fairy tales because, for her, reading and magic always went together. How do you feel about the incorporation of magical elements in a narrative? What do you think of the concept of magical realism in literature?

· ·

question 28

Hoffman claims that survival is the subject matter of her books. What do you
think she means by this?

· ·

$\cdot$ $\cdot$ $\cdot$ $\cdot$ $\cdot$ $\cdot$ $\cdot$ $\cdot$ $\cdot$ $\cdot$ $\cdot$ $\cdot$ $\cdot$ $\cdot$ $\cdot$ $\cdot$ $\cdot$ $\cdot$ $\cdot$ $\cdot$ $\cdot$ $\cdot$ $\cdot$ $\cdot$ $\cdot$ $\cdot$ $\cdot$ $\cdot$ $\cdot$

question 29

Hoffman has written books on different themes over the years. What kind of theme would you like to see her explore in her next book, and why?

$\cdot$ $\cdot$ $\cdot$ $\cdot$ $\cdot$ $\cdot$ $\cdot$ $\cdot$ $\cdot$ $\cdot$ $\cdot$ $\cdot$ $\cdot$ $\cdot$ $\cdot$ $\cdot$ $\cdot$ $\cdot$ $\cdot$ $\cdot$ $\cdot$ $\cdot$ $\cdot$ $\cdot$ $\cdot$ $\cdot$ $\cdot$ $\cdot$ $\cdot$

. . . .

question 30

Hoffman has written several widely acclaimed books, and a couple of them have been made into movies. Which book would you like to see made into a movie, and why?

. . . .

. . . .

question 31

Rachel was a Jewish woman constrained by the laws of her religion and community, forced to abide by them by her mother and other women. She rebelled against them and paid for it. How do you think Rachel's life would have turned out if she had been born as a black woman?

. . . .

. . . .

question 32

The Jewish women's association, Blessings and Peace and Loving Deeds,
kept a hawk eye on those who made a misstep, even if it was none of their
business. They justified it as "staying together because of persecution."
Would the togetherness of a persecuted community be compromised if the
members had the individual freedom to be happy and make their own
decisions? Discuss.

. . . .

question 33

Camille's expenses were paid for by his parents, who finally realized he was not going to join the business while he painted. If his parents had not been rich, how do you think Camille could have supported himself and his family?

. . . .

question 34

Lydia was a vague character, but she seemed happy with her life in Paris. How do you think she would have turned out if she had been brought up by her mother, Jestine, in St. Thomas?

. . . .

. . . .

question 35

Rachel mocked and mistreated the one son she claimed to love the most. If you were Rachel, how would you have dealt with a child you loved a lot if they chose a path in life of which you disapproved?

. . . .

. . . .

question 36

If you had to live the life of one of the characters in the book, which one would it be, and why? If the choice were to be restricted to the two women, Rachel and Jestine, whom would you prefer to be, and why?

. . . .

. . . .

question 37

Madame Halevy was a self-righteous woman who stood up for the traditions and customs that oppressed her and those around her. She disliked Rachel because she wanted something more than the restricted Jewish life the island had to offer. If you were Madame Halevy, how would you have treated Rachel, your best friend's child?

. . . .

. . . .

question 38

On the island, Europeans, Jews, and Blacks lived together, though separately. If you were to live in St. Thomas, which gender, class, and race would you prefer to have been born in, and why?

. . . .

Quiz Questions

question 39

The protagonist of the book is _____.

. . . .

question 40

_____ is Rachel's best friend.

. . . .

question 41

Camille marries _____.

question 42

Camille is considered the Father of _____.

question 43

True or false: Lydia's family is ostracized when she was known to be Jestine's daughter.

. . . .

question 44

Rachel was forced to marry _____.

. . . .

question 45

Rachel's mother was best friends with _____.

question 46

Hoffman completed her MA in creative writing from_____.

question 47

Hoffman helped establish the _____.

question 48

Hoffman wrote the screenplay for _____ .

question 49

True or false: Hoffman's first book was *The Marriage of Opposites*.

. . . .

question 50

Hoffman is influenced by_____ in her writing.

. . . .

Quiz Answers

1. Rachel Pomié
2. Jestine
3. Julie Vellay
4. Impressionism
5. True
6. Isaac Petit.
7. Madame Halevy
8. Stanford University
9. Hoffman Breast Center
10. Independence Day (1983)
11. False; Her first book was called *Property Of*, a novel based on the gangs of New York.
12. Fairy tales

THE END

Want to promote your book group? Register here.

PLEASE LEAVE US A FEEDBACK.

THANK YOU!

  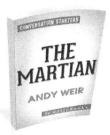

Printed in Great Britain
by Amazon

78187140R00041